This Scissor Skill
Belongs to

_____

COLOR AND CUT

A Preschool Workbook for Kids

PRACTICE LINES

Cut along the dotted lines. Keep going!

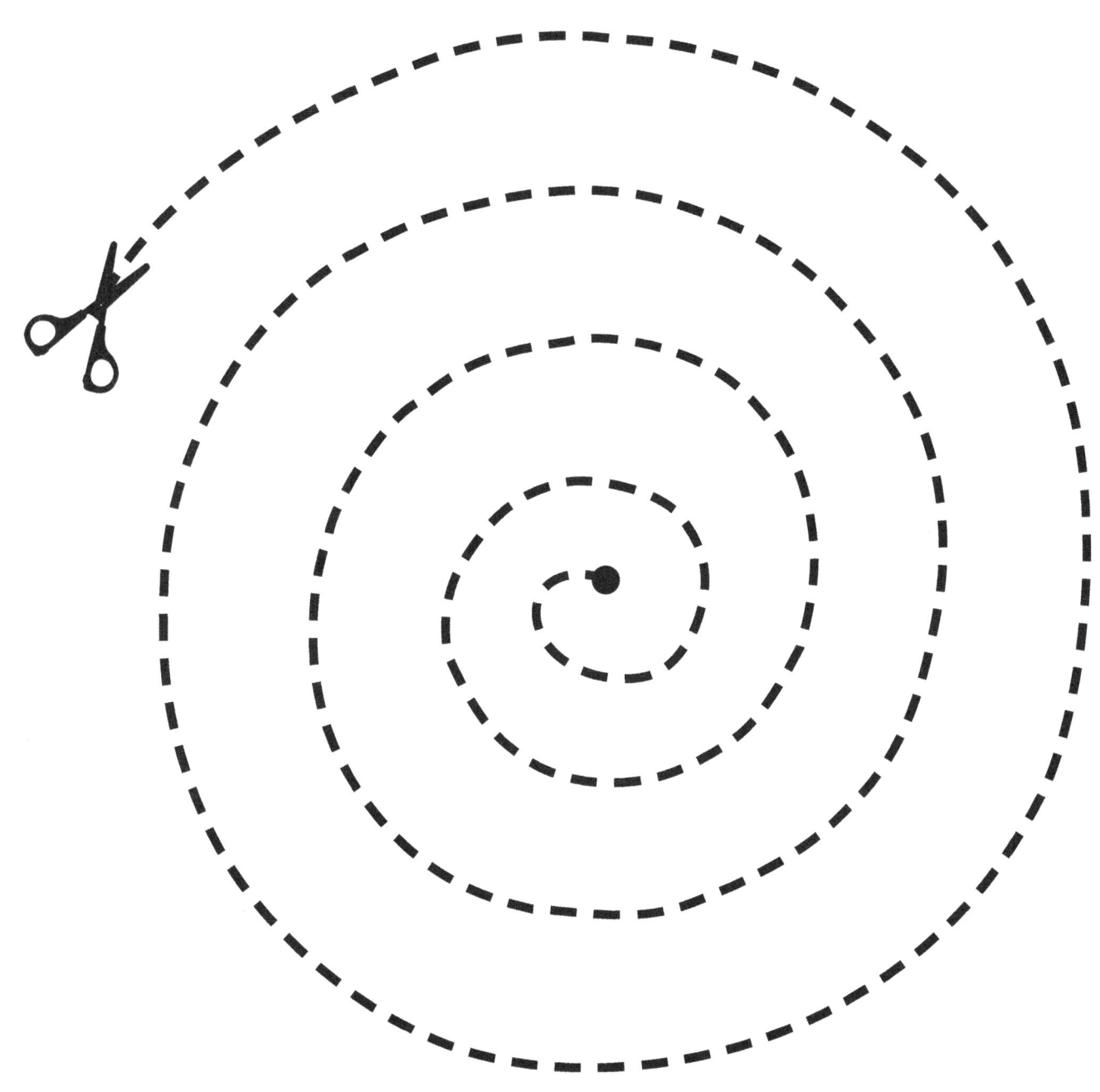

COLOR AND CUT

COLOR AND CUT

COLOR AND CUT

PRACTICE LINES

Cut along the dotted lines. Keep going!

COLOR AND CUT

COLOR AND CUT

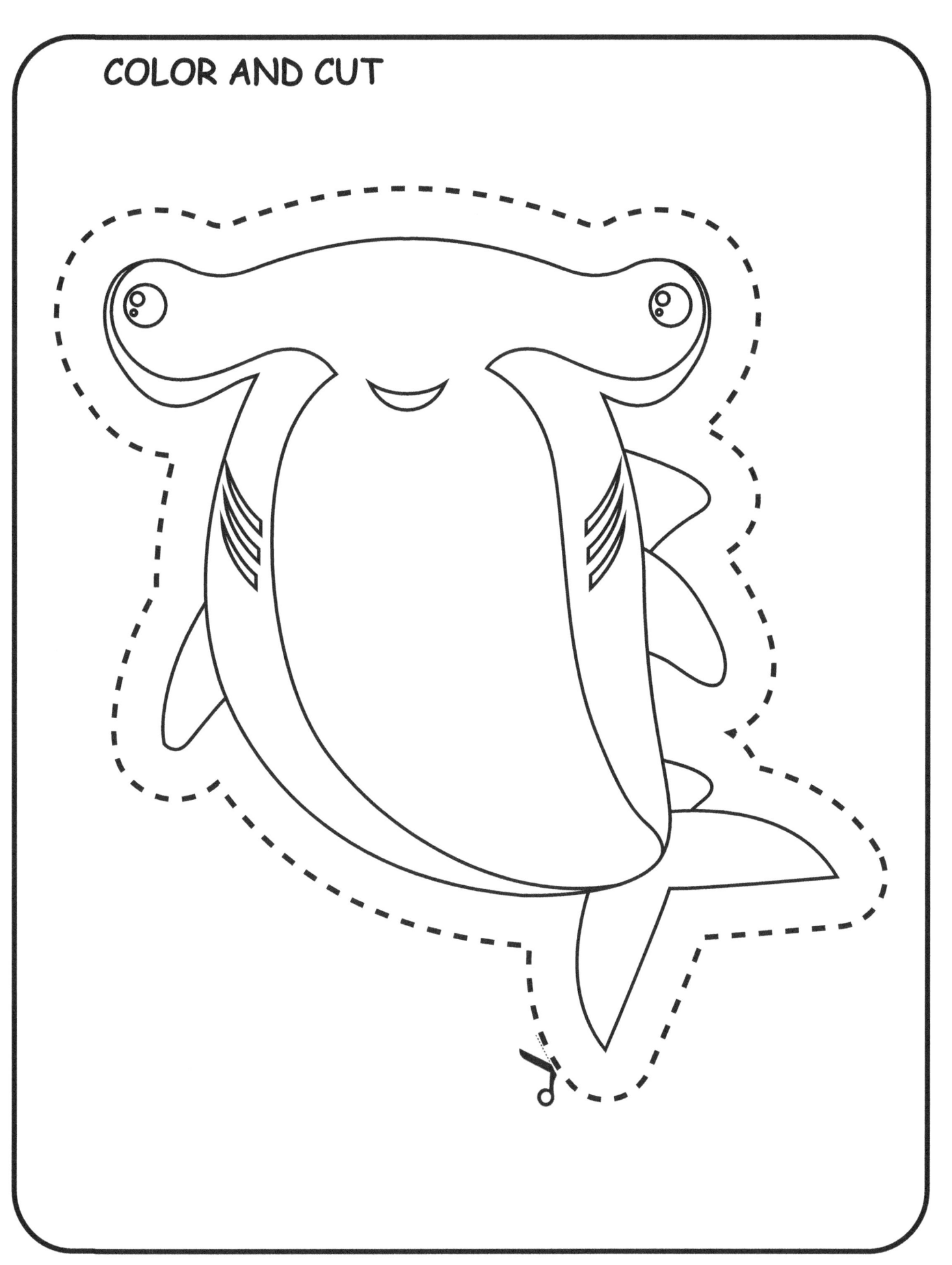

COLOR AND CUT

COLOR AND CUT

COLOR AND CUT

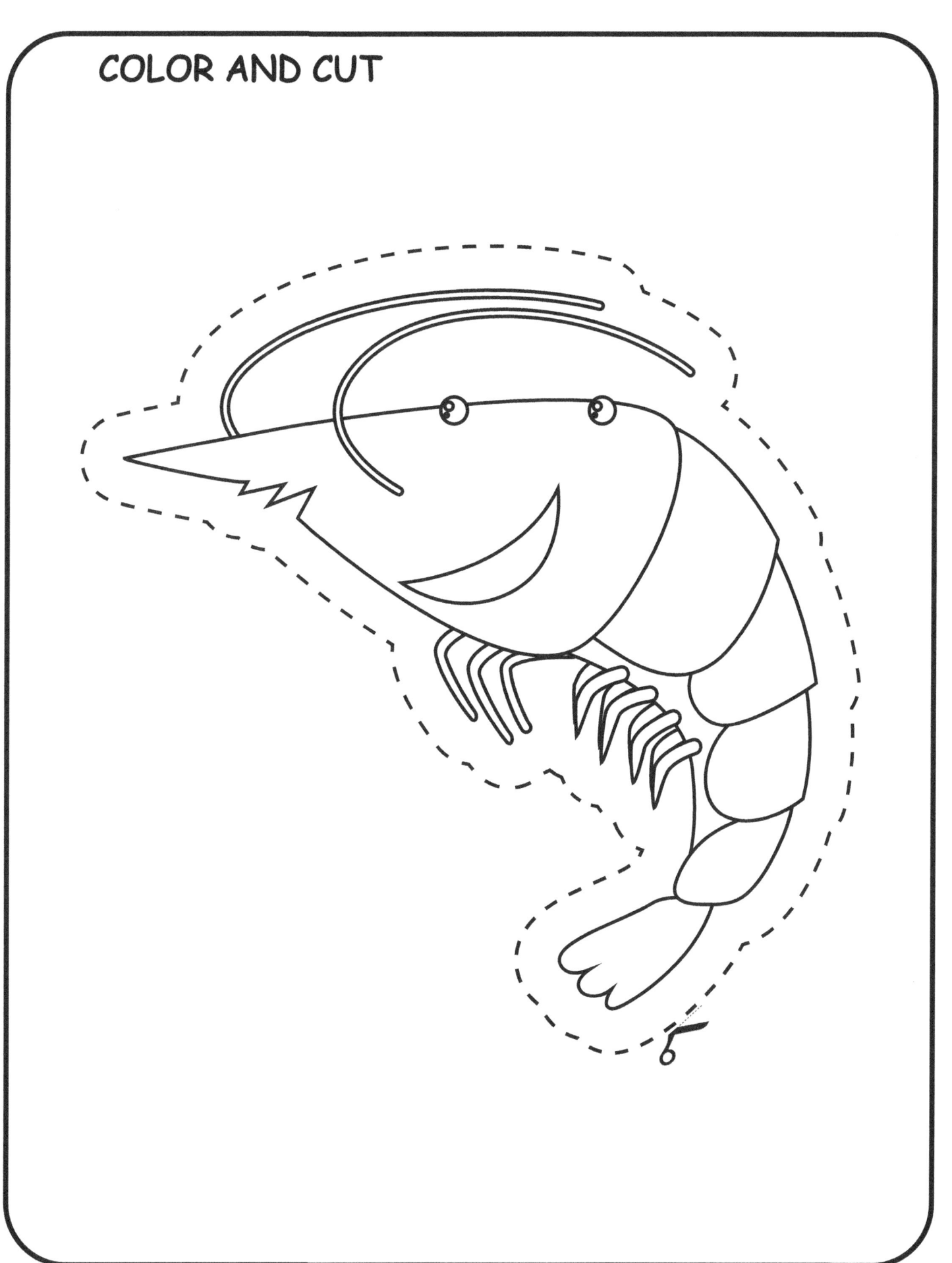

COLOR AND CUT

COLOR AND CUT

COLOR AND CUT

COLOR AND CUT

COLOR AND CUT

COLOR AND CUT

COLOR AND CUT

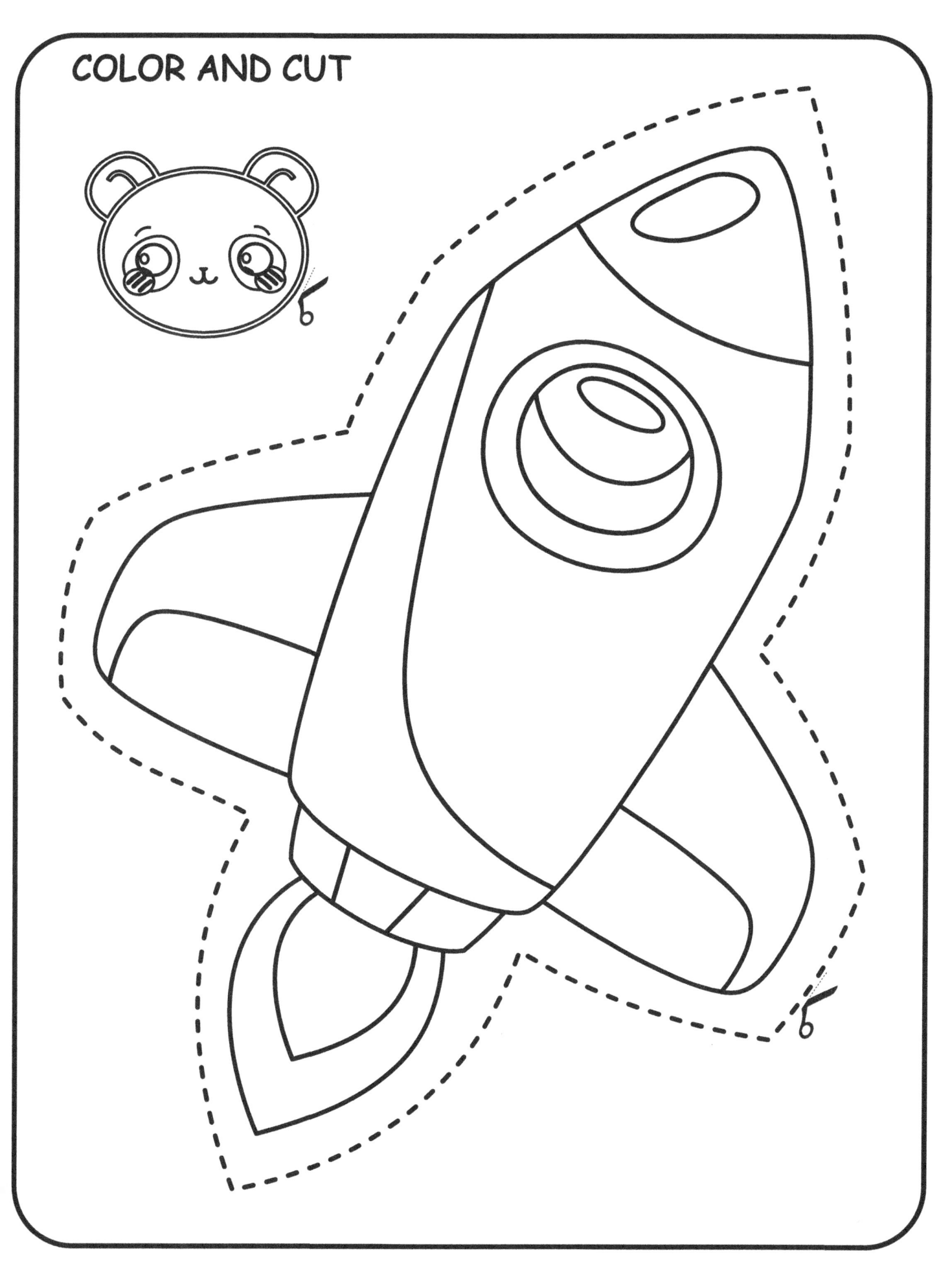

CUT AND GLUE

A Special Request.
Your brief Amazon review could really help us.
BurunduXX-Factory Publishing
THANK YOU!
Copyright © 2021 Torsten Lorenz
All rights reserved.
Cover design by Torsten Lorenz
Pinterest: BigLoro.redbubble.com
Contact: Torsten Lorenz
Theresienstrasse 10
01097 Dresden Germany
burunduxx-factory@gmx.de

Made in the USA
Monee, IL
17 May 2022